EARLY SKILLS LIBRARY

writing skills

Developed by Macmillan Educational Company
Written by Carol Vejvoda Murdock
Text illustrated by Doug Cushman
Cover illustrated by Patrick Girouard

Newbridge Educational Programs

TABLE OF CONTENTS

TABLE OF CONTENTS
Continued

TERRIFIC TRACING
Drawing Shapes

This activity gives children practice in making the writing motions used to form many letters.

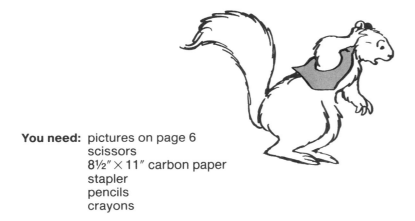

You need: pictures on page 6
scissors
8½″ × 11″ carbon paper
stapler
pencils
crayons

Steps:

1. Reproduce the pictures on page 6 for each child.

2. Cut several 8½″ × 11″ pieces of carbon paper in half to make 8½″ × 5½″ sections. Make one carbon paper section for each child in your class.

3. Give each child a copy of the pictures and a carbon paper section. Ask children to cut apart the pictures on the dotted lines. Have each child create a "sandwich" with the picture and carbon paper, placing the picture of a circus clown on the bottom, the carbon paper (pigmented side down) in the middle, and the picture of various shapes on top.

4. Align the black dots on the pictures and staple together each child's sandwiched paper at the top center.

5. Pressing hard with pencils, children will trace the various shapes shown in the picture on top. Remind children to trace the circles counterclockwise, following the arrows. Children will trace the lines from left to right.

6. When children have traced each shape, have them remove the top paper and the carbon paper to reveal the finished clown picture.

7. Let children color their completed pictures.

Step 3

Step 5

Name _____

ANIMAL OUTLINES
Worksheet

Find the five animals hiding in the picture below.
With a pencil, trace the dotted lines.
Then color in the whole picture.

Name______________________________

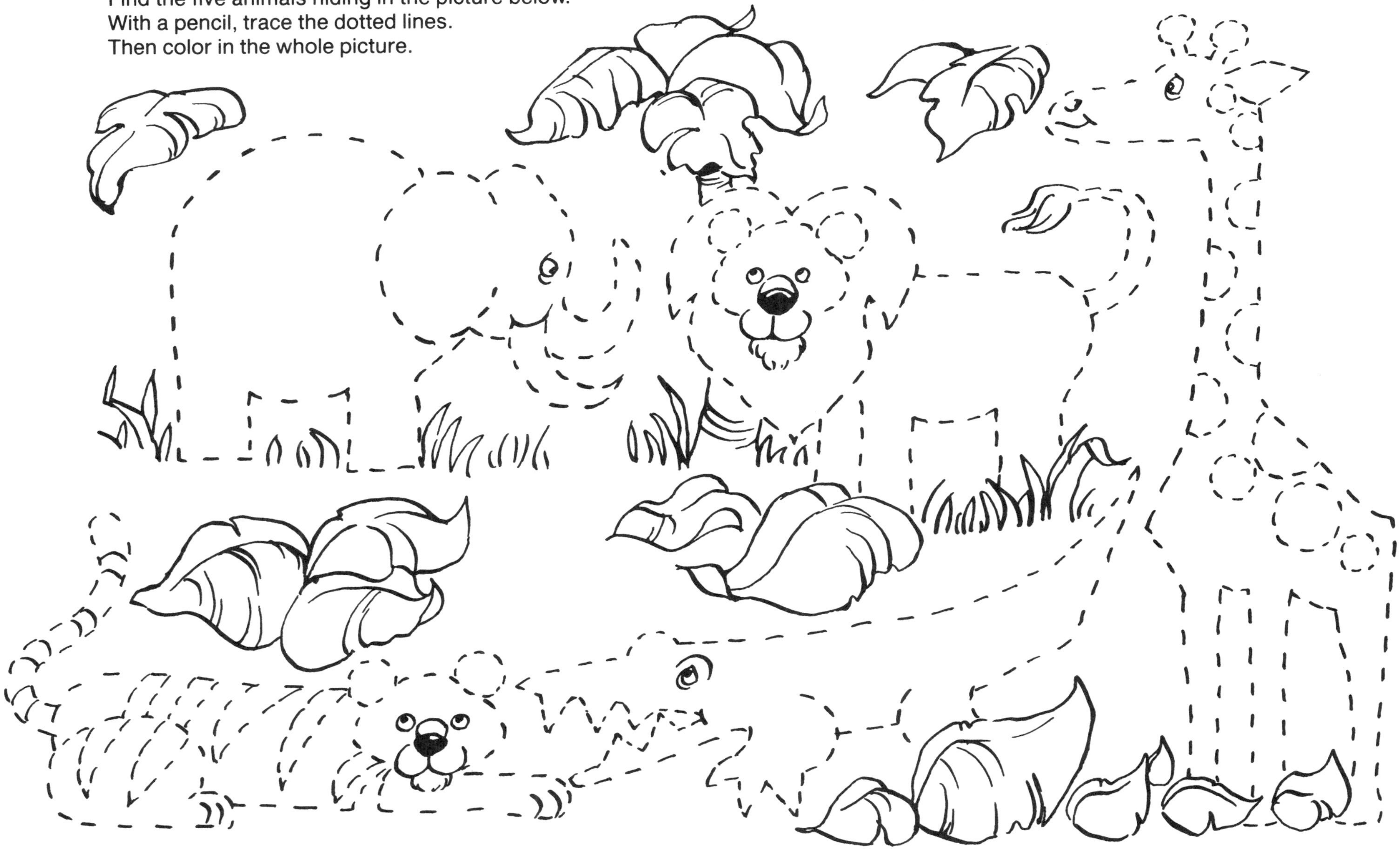

Trace the dotted lines to make the letters.
Then, on the lines, write the letters on your own.

Name_____

Trace the dotted lines to make the letters.
Then, on the lines, write the letters on your own.

Trace the dotted lines to make the letters.
Then, on the lines, write the letters on your own.

Name_____

PIRATE ISLAND

Trace the dotted lines to make the letters.
Then, on the lines, write the letters on your own.

Name_____

LETTER TRACINGS
Worksheet

Trace the dotted lines to make the letters.
Then, on the lines, write the letters on your own.

Name_____

LETTER TRACINGS
Worksheet

Trace the dotted lines to make the letters.
Then, on the lines, write the letters on your own.

Name_____

LETTER TRACINGS
Worksheet

Trace the dotted lines to make the letters.
Then, on the lines, write the letters on your own.

Name________________________

M M

m m

N N

n n

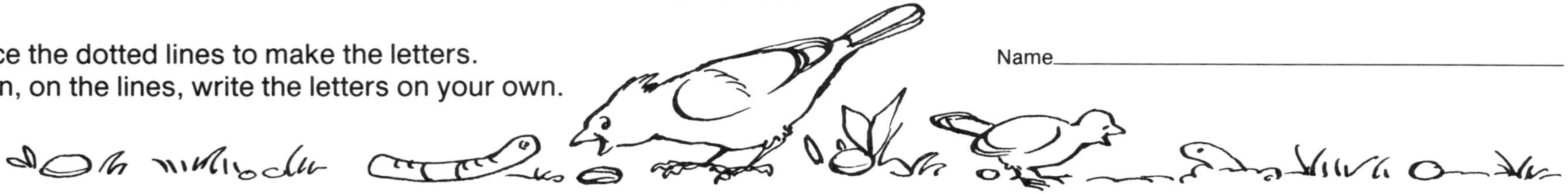

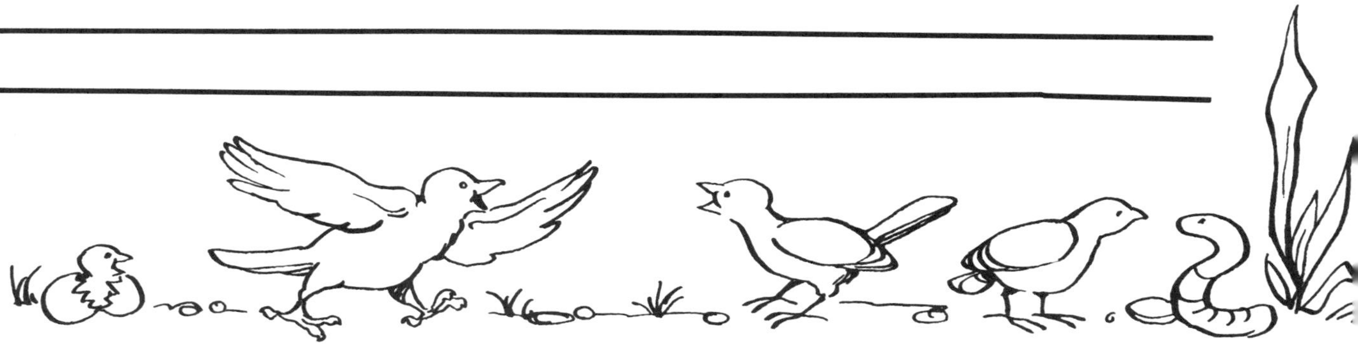

Trace the dotted lines to make the letters.
Then, on the lines, write the letters on your own.

Name

Trace the dotted lines to make the letters.
Then, on the lines, write the letters on your own.

Name_____

Trace the dotted lines to make the letters.
Then, on the lines, write the letters on your own.

Name_____

S S

S S

I I

I I

Trace the dotted lines to make the letters.
Then, on the lines, write the letters on your own.

Name_____

Trace the dotted lines to make the letters.
Then, on the lines, write the letters on your own.

Name_____

LETTER TRACINGS
Worksheet

Trace the dotted lines to make the letters.
Then, on the lines, write the letters on your own.

Name_____

LETTER LEARNING
Writing Activity

To give students practice in tracing and writing capital and lowercase letters,
use the suggested writing activity below.

You need: worksheets on pages 22 and 23
clear plastic adhesive
crayons or grease pencils
damp paper towels

Steps:

1. Reproduce copies of the letter worksheets on pages 22 and 23.

2. Cover the worksheets with clear plastic adhesive, or you may laminate them.

3. Distribute the worksheets to the children, along with crayons or grease pencils.

4. Allow the children to watch you draw each lowercase or uppercase letter on the chalkboard. As you draw each letter, have children trace the letter on their worksheets and then write the letter on their own in the spaces provided.

5. After children have finished, their worksheets may be wiped clean with damp paper towels and reused at another time.

Variation:

Instead of reproducing enough worksheets for all the children in the class, make only one copy of each worksheet, laminate or cover with clear plastic adhesive, and tape the worksheets to a special desk set aside in a writing corner. Allow children to spend time at this desk to practice writing the letters of the alphabet. The worksheets may be wiped clean so that other children may use the writing desk at other times.

BIG LETTERS ON THE LOOSE
Worksheet

With a crayon, trace each letter, one at a time. After you trace one letter,
write the same letter on your own, in the space next to each letter.

Name _____

A B C D E

F G H I J K

L M N O P

Q R S T U

V W X Y Z

With a crayon, trace each letter, one at a time. After you trace one letter, write the same letter on your own, in the space next to each letter.

Name _____

Use the letter game described below to give children practice in writing
the capital letters and lowercase letters of the alphabet.

You need: copies of the bingo game boards on
this page and page 25
clear plastic adhesive (or you may laminate)
crayons or grease pencils

BINGO!

Steps:

1. Make copies of the bingo game boards on this page and on page
25, and distribute one to each child. If desired, laminate game
boards or cover them with clear plastic adhesive so that they may
be wiped clean and used again. Cut the boards apart.

2. On the chalkboard, write the capital and lowercase of a letter of the
alphabet and say the letter aloud. Tell children to check their game
boards. If they have the dotted outlines of that capital and lowercase letter, they must trace the outlines with a crayon or a grease
pencil. Continue writing and calling out letters until one or several
of the children complete their game boards. (Note: G, P, Q, and Y
do not appear on the boards.)

3. To win, a child must have completely filled in his or her game board
and correctly traced the dotted outlines of the letters that you have
written on the chalkboard.

Variations:

1. Give children more than one game board. In order to win, children
must complete all of their game boards.

2. Using oaktag and fine-line markers, create more game boards for
variety.

W	w
R	r
K	k
V	v

D	d
E	e
B	b
A	a

L	l
B	b
R	r
D	d

M	m
N	n
Z	z
H	h

T	t
U	u
V	v
W	w

M	m
C	c
D	d
L	l

E	e
I	i
R	r
H	h

Z	z
K	k
N	n
F	f

Reproduce the worksheet on page 28 for your class. As you read aloud the story below, emphasize the underlined color words. Have children color in the pictures on the worksheet, following the color words contained in the story.

ONCE upon a time there was a little girl who lived with her mother in the forest. She was called Little Red Riding Hood, because she always wore the <u>red</u> velvet cloak her grandmother had made for her. One day, Red Riding Hood's mother asked her to take a pretty cake with <u>pink</u> icing to her grandmother's house. So Red Riding Hood put the cake into a big, <u>yellow</u> basket, buttoned up her <u>red</u> cloak, and started off through the woods to her grandmother's house.

On her way, Red Riding Hood met a big, <u>black</u> wolf.

"What a lovely <u>red</u> cloak you have, my dear," said the big, <u>black</u> wolf.

"Thank you," she replied.

"Would you like me to help you carry that big, <u>yellow</u> basket?"

"No, thank you, kind wolf. My mother told me I must bring it to my grandmother's house myself."

"And where does your grandmother live, dear girl?"

"She lives on the other side of these tall, <u>green</u> trees."

"Aha," said the wolf to himself. "I'll run as fast as I can, and get to the grandmother's house before Red Riding Hood. Then I can gobble up the grandmother *and* the little girl!"

"Well, good day then, Red Riding Hood. I'll let you go on your way."

So Little Red Riding Hood tripped merrily along through the woods until she came to her grandmother's house. When she arrived at her grandmother's house, she knocked gently at the front door.

"Come in, dearie," said a voice from inside. Red Riding Hood stepped into the house, and there she saw her grandmother lying in bed, all tucked in under her bright <u>blue</u> blanket. And on her head, she wore a frilly, <u>purple</u> nightcap.

"Oh, my, grandmother, how different you look today."

"That's because I haven't been feeling well, my dear."

"But, grandmother, what big, <u>green</u> eyes you have."

"The better to see you with, my girl."

"And, grandmother, what large, <u>black</u> ears you have."

"The better to hear you with, my dear."

"But grandmother, what a big, <u>black</u> nose you have."

"The better to smell what you've brought me, my sweet."

"Oh, my," said Little Red Riding Hood, "what great big, <u>yellow</u> teeth you have, grandmother."

"The better to eat you with, my pretty." And with that the big, <u>black</u> wolf leapt out of the bed and chased Red Riding Hood around the house, grabbing at her pretty, <u>red</u> velvet cloak.

"Oh dear, oh dear," cried Little Red Riding Hood.

"I've got you now," growled the big, <u>black</u> wolf. But just at that moment, a passing hunter walked by the cottage and saw the wolf chasing Red Riding Hood.

The hunter rushed into the grandmother's cottage and killed the big, <u>black</u> wolf with his ax. Then he chopped off the lock of the closet door, and found Little Red Riding Hood's grandmother tied up on the floor. The brave hunter freed the grandmother and gave her some water, since she was quite thirsty after being in the closet for so long.

Little Red Riding Hood stood on the tip of her toes and kissed the brave hunter on his <u>brown</u>, leathery face.

"Oh, thank you," she cried, "you have saved our lives. How can we ever thank you?"

"It is thanks enough to know that you and your grandmother are safe, my dear. And now that the bad wolf can never hurt you again, I must be on my way." And with a tip of his bright <u>green</u> cap, he left the cottage and returned to the woods. Then Little Red Riding Hood gave her grandmother the special cake that her mother had baked, and returned to her house at the other end of the woods. And you can be sure that she didn't stop to talk to any more wolves on her way home.

Follow-up Activity:

Explain to children that using color words in the story makes it more vivid and interesting and gives the listeners a better idea of what the setting of the story looks like.

Listen to the story of Little Red Riding Hood.
Color each of the pictures with the colors that you hear in the story.

Name _____

To give children practice in identifying nouns, adjectives, and verbs, make the picture wordbook described below.

You need: magazines
scissors
9″ × 12″ construction paper
(five sheets per child)
glue
markers
stapler
crayons

Steps:

1. From magazines, have each child cut out ten pictures of people, animals, or objects.

2. Tell the children to fold their sheets of construction paper in half, lengthwise, and glue one picture onto each inside half.

3. Have the children write beneath each picture (or dictate to you) the noun that identifies it. Then ask children to think of a word that describes the noun (e.g., fat, big, yellow, and so on) and write it under the noun.

4. Bind the pages of the wordbooks by stapling the folded sheets together along the folds.

5. Have the children color the cover of their wordbooks, and help them write an appropriate title on the cover (e.g., *Animal Wordbook, People Wordbook, People and Things Wordbook,* and so on).

6. Allow the children to exchange the wordbooks with their classmates to expand their vocabularies.

Variations:

1. Ask children to look for pictures of things for each letter of the alphabet. Then have children write each letter of the alphabet above the picture and the word for each below the picture. Tell children to alphabetize the pictures and bind the pages together to make a picture dictionary.

2. Have the children look for pictures of things that rhyme (e.g., a cat/a hat, a man/a can, a boy/a toy, a rope/soap, and so on) to place on the halves of their wordbook pages.

3. Tell the children to look for pictures of people, animals, or things in motion. Instead of having the children write nouns, ask them to write the action words that describe what is going on in the pictures (e.g., eating, swimming, driving, smiling, sailing, playing, and so on).

Use the writing activity below to give children practice in writing short poems.

You need: 12″ × 18″ construction paper
(one sheet per child)
pencils, colored markers, or crayons
lined paper (one sheet per child)

Name Rhyming

Little stars ☆
In my eyes 👁
Nice and fair 🙂
Doesn't cry
Adorable am I

Friendly smile 🙂
Red hair. 💡
Extra smart
Don't like to share

Steps:

1. Give each child a piece of construction paper and pencils, colored markers, or crayons.

2. Tell children to write their names in capital letters down the left side of the paper. (For younger children, write a sample name vertically on the chalkboard.)

3. On a sheet of lined paper, have children write words that describe themselves. (Younger children may dictate words to you.)

4. Explain to the children that they are going to write a poem about themselves, using the descriptive words. Each line of the poem must begin with a letter in their names. They can compose the poems on the lined paper. (Younger children may dictate their poems to you.)

5. Once the poems are complete, have children write them on the construction paper, and illustrate them in the remaining space.

6. Display the illustrated name-rhymes on a bulletin board labeled "Name Rhyming," or on a classroom wall.

Follow-up Activity:

Read the rhymes aloud to the class to see if children can figure out who wrote each one.

Variations:

1. Younger children may simply think of descriptive words about themselves that begin with each letter of their names. Children may then write the words on construction paper beside each letter of their names, or dictate them for you to write.

2. Instead of using the letters in their names, let children use the names of the months in which they were born, the name of a season or holiday, or the name of their astrological signs as the starting point for their rhymes.

RHYMING-WORD GAME
Classroom Game / Writing Activity

Use the rhyming game described below to introduce children to rhyming words.

You need: rhyming-word game cards on pages 32 and 33
rhyming-word game boards on pages 34 and 35
oaktag
scissors
pencils
lined paper
crayons

Optional: clear plastic
adhesive

Steps:

1. Reproduce the rhyming-word cards several times. Reproduce the rhyming-word game boards several times.

2. Mount the word cards and game boards on oaktag. Laminate them or cover them with clear plastic adhesive. Then cut apart the word cards and the game boards along the dotted lines.

3. Shuffle the word cards and place them facedown in a pile in the center of the play area.

4. Give each child a game board. (Younger children may play in pairs.) The youngest child will be the first player.

5. Each player will draw a card from the card pile. If he or she has a word on the game board that rhymes with the word on the card, the player will place that card on one of the rhyming squares of game board. If the player does not have a word that rhymes with the one drawn, place the card at the bottom of the card pile.

6. Play continues clockwise until a child covers one row of rhyming words.

7. When a player has completed a row of rhyming words, while play continues have the child make up a four-line rhyme using either set of four rhyming words on his or her game board.

Follow-up Activity:

After a number of children have made up rhymes, have them write the poems (or dictate them to you) and draw illustrations to accompany the poems.

Variations:

1. For younger children, allow the winner to make up a two-line poem with two rhyming words from his or her game board.

2. Cut apart the game boards and use the word squares as additional cards. Combine all of the word cards and place them facedown to play a concentration game. Each child in turn picks two cards. If the words on them rhyme, the cards are set aside. If they do not, the cards are put facedown again. The idea is to remember which words are where. The player with the most pairs of rhyming words will win.

bear

chair

square

pear

hat

cat

bat

rat

bed

sled

head

bread

pie

eye

tie

Y

key	bee	tree	flea
fan	man	can	pan
eel	seal	wheel	meal
whale	tail	jail	snail

RHYMING-WORD GAME
Game Boards

see	hair	feel	thread
sea	care	real	red
knee	pair	peel	dead
pea	share	deal	fed

mail	tan	sat	sky
rail	ran	that	shy
sail	van	mat	sigh
fail	than	fat	fly

CURDIE AND THE GOBLINS
Story Adapted from a Welsh Legend

Reproduce the coloring worksheet on the following page, one for each child in the class. Then, read aloud the story below, repeating each paragraph. The first time you read aloud each paragraph, omit the descriptive phrases in parentheses. Then tell children to listen carefully as you reread each paragraph, including the descriptive phrases in parentheses. Ask children to color in their worksheets based on the descriptive phrases used in the story.

LONG ago in the land of Wales, there lived a very brave young man named Curdie. Curdie was a miner. All day long he worked deep down under the ground in the *(long, narrow, echoing)* tunnels of a mine, digging out lumps of coal with his pickax. Curdie was known as the bravest miner in all of Wales.

In a *(deep, dark, slimy)* cave beneath the mine there lived a band of evil goblins. One night these goblins set out to kidnap the beautiful princess, Gwendolyn, from her bedroom in the royal palace. The goblins had dug a *(long, narrow, echoing)* tunnel that reached all the way from their cave straight up to the princess's bedroom. They crept *(slyly, sneakily, and silently)* through that tunnel and burst into the princess's bedroom. The goblins grabbed the sleeping princess and carried her off to their *(deep, dark, slimy)* cave beneath the mine.

The queen, who was a very wise woman, sent for Curdie as soon as she discovered that the princess was missing. When Curdie arrived at the palace, the queen led him to the princess's bedroom. In the middle of the floor was the opening to the *(long, narrow, echoing)* tunnel.

"Curdie, you are the bravest miner in the land, and only you can rescue my daughter. But be careful," she warned, "for the goblins are very dangerous. To help you escape from their *(deep, dark, slimy)* cave, take this ball of magic thread. Unwind it as you crawl through the *(long, narrow, echoing)* tunnel, so that you can find your way back to the palace." And the queen handed Curdie a big ball of *(shining, silvery, magical)* thread. At once, Curdie climbed down into the tunnel to rescue the princess.

Deeper and deeper into the tunnel walked Curdie. He got closer and closer to the goblins' *(deep, dark, slimy)* cave. As he walked, Curdie unwound the ball of *(shining, silvery, magical)* thread that the queen had given him.

Suddenly, Curdie stopped. Ahead of him shone a strange *(flickering, eerie, evil-looking)* light. Curdie inched forward on tiptoe. As he came closer to the light, he saw four of the meanest-looking goblins sitting in a circle. The first goblin looked like an old *(lumpy, stumpy, bumpy)* potato. The second goblin looked like the *(twirly, twisting, curly)* roots of an old tree. The third goblin looked like a fat *(wishy, squishy, squirmy)* worm. And the fourth goblin looked like a big *(hairy, scary, snarly)* bear. In the center of the circle sat the fair princess, Gwendolyn.

With a great cry, Curdie sprang forward and whisked the princess away. They both ran as fast as they could. The goblins began to scream and shout. They made such a dreadful noise that the walls of the cave shook and trembled. Then there was a loud cracking sound, and the walls of the *(deep, dark, slimy)* cave came tumbling down on the evil goblins.

Curdie and the princess couldn't see a thing except the *(shining, silvery, magical)* thread. Following the outstretched thread, Curdie and the princess found their way back to the palace. Upon their return, a great feast was prepared for them, and everyone in the town celebrated their safe return.

Discussion Questions:
1. What kind of tunnels did Curdie work in and did the goblins dig?
2. What did the goblins' cave look like?
3. What did the ball of thread look like?
4. Describe the four mean-looking goblins.
5. Discuss with children how the descriptive phrases add interest and excitement to the story.

CURDIE AND THE GOBLINS
Worksheet

Listen carefully to the story of Curdie and the Goblins.
After you have heard the story, color in the picture below.

Name _____

Make the flannel-board patterns on page 40 to use when you tell this story to your class. Emphasize the pronouns used in the story. Then ask children the questions following the story. Encourage them to use the pronouns <u>he</u>, <u>she</u>, and <u>they</u>.

ONE cool spring morning, Rosie Robin was hopping around on the ground, looking for good things to eat. Suddenly, right in front of her beak, Wally Worm popped out of the ground. "What a nice, fat worm," thought Rosie, and <u>she</u> tried to pull Wally out of the ground.

"No! No!" cried Wally as <u>he</u> tried to pull away from Rosie. <u>He</u> pulled. <u>She</u> pulled. <u>They</u> both pulled as hard as <u>they</u> could.

Just then, four more robins came hopping by—Ruby Robin and Ramona Robin and Richie Robin and Rudy Robin. <u>They</u> all wanted to help. So Rudy took hold of Richie, and <u>he</u> took hold of Ramona, and <u>she</u> took hold of Ruby, and <u>she</u> took hold of Rosie, and <u>they</u> all pulled together. <u>They</u> pulled and <u>they</u> pulled.

Things looked bad for Wally, but down in the ground, four of his wiggly friends came to the rescue—Willie Worm and Wendy Worm and Winnie Worm and Wesley Worm. How could they help Wally? Well, Wesley took hold of Winnie, and <u>she</u> took hold of Wendy, and <u>she</u> took hold of Willie, and <u>he</u> took hold of Wally, and <u>they</u> all pulled together. <u>They</u> pulled and <u>they</u> pulled. The robins pulled one way and the worms pulled the other way. Poor Wally, who was in the middle, was getting quite stretched out of shape.

At last, Rudy Robin grew tired of pulling.

"This is not my worm," <u>he</u> said, and <u>he</u> flew away.

"Nor mine," said Richie, and <u>he</u> flew away.

"Nor mine," said Ramona, and <u>she</u> flew away.

"Nor mine," said Ruby, and <u>she</u> flew away.

That left Rosie all by herself, pulling against all those worms. Rosie looked at Wally and thought: "<u>He</u> does not look so very fat anyway!" So <u>she</u> let go of Wally and flew away to find something easier to eat.

What happened to Wally? <u>He</u> tumbled right back into the ground on top of Willie and Wendy and Winnie and Wesley. For a moment <u>they</u> all lay there, tangled up with each other. Then <u>they</u> all wiggled away to get on with the day.

Discussion Questions:

1. What did Rosie do when she saw Wally?

2. How did Ruby, Ramona, Richie, and Rudy try to help Rosie?

3. What did Wally's friends do to help him?

4. When Rosie's friends got tired, what did they do?

5. What did Wally and his friends do after Rosie flew away?

FLANNEL BOARD

You need: robin and worm patterns on page 40
scissors
glue
oaktag
crayons or colored markers
felt scraps

THE ROBIN–WORM TUG OF WAR

You need: chalk
gloves or mittens (two for each child)
clothesline ropes (12′ long)

Steps:

1. Reproduce the robin and worm patterns on page 40 three times each, and cut them out.

2. You will need three female robins and two male robins, and three male worms and two female worms. Mount them on oaktag and cut them out. If desired, color the robins and worms or have the children color them.

3. With a dark marker, write the names of the robins and worms on the patterns, so that children will easily be able to identify which ones are male and which are female.

4. Glue small scraps of felt to the backs of the patterns. Then use the flannel-board patterns to help you tell the story of Rosie Robin and Wally Worm.

Variation:

Reproduce the patterns, trace them directly onto felt, and cut them out. Decorate the felt creatures with markers, and glue small bows of ribbon onto the female robins and worms to help children identify the creatures easily.

Steps:

1. On the playground, draw two parallel chalk lines, about 14′ long and 5′ apart.

2. Divide your class into groups of five so that there is and even number of groups of robins and groups of worms. (If the class does not divide evenly, have the remaining children help you judge the tug-of-war contest.)

3. Have the children put on their gloves or mittens. Then ask the robin groups to line up behind one of the chalk lines and have the worm groups line up behind the other chalk line.

4. Give each opposing set of robins and worms a clothesline. When you give the starting signal, have the robins and worms tug at the clotheslines. The first group of each set of robins and worms to pull its opposing group across its own chalk line is the winner.

Follow-up Activity:

After the tug-of-war contests, encourage children to describe their contests, using full sentences that contain the pronouns *he, she,* and *they.*

THE WALLOWING, SWALLOWING WHALE
Action Story

Read this story to your class. Then play the games on page 43 to give children practice in creating simple sentences.

THERE once was a wallowing, swallowing whale who lived in the deep, dark sea. All day and all night he swam and swam *[make swimming motions with arms]* through the walloping waves. As he swam, he swallowed *[open and close hand like a mouth swallowing]* everything in sight.

One day, as he was wallowing and swallowing along, he saw a sailor *[shade eyes with hand]* on a raft. He opened his jaws wide and swallowed the sailor *[open and close hand like a mouth swallowing]*, raft and all!

The wallowing, swallowing whale swam on and on *[make swimming motions with arms]* until he saw a boy and a girl in a sailboat *[shade eyes with hand]*. With a great gulp, he swallowed them up *[open and close hand like a mouth swallowing]*, sailboat and all!

The wallowing, swallowing whale swam along through the walloping waves *[make swimming motions with arms]*. In a little while he saw *[shade eyes with hand]* a dog dog-paddling in the water *[move hands as if dog-paddling]*. And he swallowed the dog *[open and close hand like a mouth swallowing]* in a single gulp!

Then the whale swam and swam some more *[make swimming motions with arms]*. Suddenly he saw *[shade eyes with hand]* a duck flying over the deep, dark sea *[make flying motions with arms]*. He opened his mouth as wide as he could and swallowed the duck *[open and close hand like a mouth swallowing]* right out of the sky!

On and on swam the whale *[make swimming motions with arms]*, feeling quite full and happy. But the sailor, the boy, the girl, the dog, and the duck who were inside the whale were not happy at all. They thought and thought, trying to figure out how to get out of the whale's stomach. After a long while, the sailor spoke.

"I have an idea *[raise one arm]*! We must make this wallowing, swallowing whale so uncomfortable that he will want to get rid of us. Now, what can each one of us do to make this whale uncomfortable?"

"I can run," said the girl *[run in place]*.

"I can clap," said the boy *[clap hands]*.

"I can bark," said the dog *[make barking sounds]*.

"I can fly," said the duck *[make flying motions with arms]*.

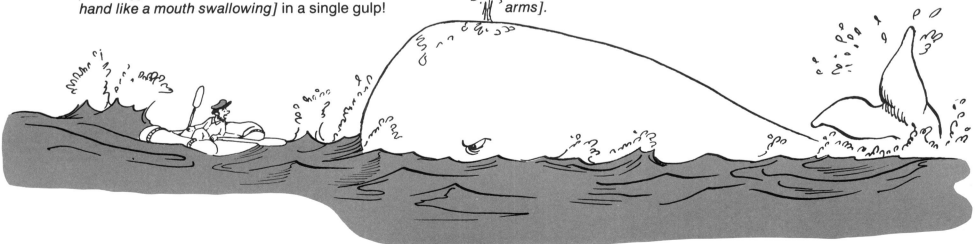

"And I can sing," said the sailor [sing "Yo Ho Ho!"].

So the girl ran [motions], the boy clapped [motions], the dog barked [sounds], the duck flew [motions], and the sailor sang [sounds].

The commotion was simply awful. Very soon the whale began to feel terrible! He shouted, "Stop that running [motions] and clapping [motions] and barking [sounds] and flying [motions] and singing [sounds]!"

The sailor yelled back, "Not until you let us out of here!"

The whale groaned and said, "Gladly! I'll give a big hiccup [hiccuping sound] and get rid of you right now!"

"Oh no!" said the sailor. "You must swim and swim until you reach land—and then you can give a big hiccup [hiccuping sound] and get rid of us."

So the girl ran [motions], the boy clapped [motions], the dog barked [sounds], the duck flew [motions], the sailor sang [sounds], and the whale swam [motions] until he reached land. Then the whale gave a big hiccup [sound], and out popped the girl, the boy, the dog, the duck, and the sailor. The whale heaved a great sigh of relief [sound] and said, "I will never, ever again swallow a girl, a boy, a dog, a duck, or a sailor." And away he swam [motions]. The girl and the boy and the dog and the duck and the sailor ran [motions] and clapped [motions] and barked [sounds] and flew [motions] and sang [sounds] one last time—just to remind that wallowing, swallowing whale to keep his promise!

THE WHALE GAME

THE DUCK FLIES!

You need: masking tape
record or tape player
record or tape of music
with a slow beat

Steps:

1. On the floor in an open area of the room, mark off a box, about 2′ square, with strips of masking tape. This is the whale's mouth.

2. Have children form a circle that passes through the whale's mouth.

3. Ask each child to choose one character who was swallowed in the story of "The Wallowing, Swallowing Whale" (the sailor, the girl, the boy, the dog, or the duck).

4. Start the music. At this signal children will walk slowly, counterclockwise in a circle, moving in time to the music.

5. As each child steps into the whale's mouth, he or she names his or her selected character and the action associated with that character. (For example: "I am the boy. The boy claps.") At the same time, the child performs the appropriate action.

6. Stop the music after a few moments. When the music stops, the child who is inside the whale's mouth is "swallowed" and must drop out of the game.

7. As the game continues, the circle gets smaller each time a player drops out. When only one child remains, the game is over.

Variation:

Make a "whale" from a large refrigerator box by cutting off the front and back ends of the box and standing it upright. Draw a large whale on each of the two remaining long sides of the box. Use the box "whale" instead of the square marked off with masking tape.

SCRAMBLED SENTENCES

You need: black marker
fourteen 3″ × 5″ unlined index cards
scissors
flannel scraps
glue
flannel board

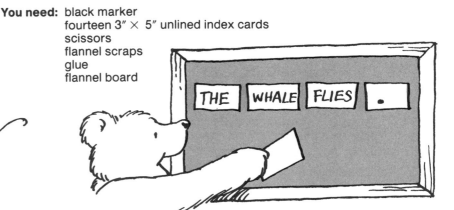

Steps:

1. With a black marker, write the following words on 3″ × 5″ unlined index cards: *The, whale, sailor, boy, girl, dog, duck, runs, claps, barks, flies, sings, swims.* On the last index card, draw a period.

2. Cut 14 small pieces of flannel and glue a piece onto the back of each index card.

3. On the left-hand side of the flannel board, put the card with the word *The.* Place the period on the right-hand side of the flannel board.

4. Separate the remaining index cards into two groups, one of nouns, and one of verbs. Place each group facedown on a desk or chair in front of the flannel board.

5. Choose one child to come to the flannel board and select a card from each pile. Have the child place the cards on the flannel board between the word *The* and the period.

6. Then read the words aloud to the class. Ask children if the words make a sentence, and, if not, how the words should be arranged to form a sentence.

7. Repeat the game, removing the noun and verb cards and letting another child place two different cards on the flannel board.

Use the sentence-making game below to give children practice in constructing sentences with the proper punctuation.

Steps:

1. Form a circle with the children.

2. To start the game, say a word that would begin a simple sentence. The child on your left should say a word to continue the sentence.

3. The game continues clockwise until the last word of the sentence has been said. The next child must then name the punctuation mark that belongs at the end of the sentence.

4. The subsequent child then begins a new sentence. If a player says a word that does not logically follow the construction of the sentence, or names an inappropriate end punctuation, he or she must drop out of the game. This is also the case if the player forgets to provide end punctuation.

5. Play the game for as long as interest continues.

Variation:

While children are playing the game, write their sentences on the chalkboard as they create them. Review the sentences with your class after the game has ended.

Use the game described below to give children practice in constructing simple sentences.

You need: clothes patterns on pages 46 and 47
scissors
construction paper (red, blue, orange, yellow, pink,
and white, 10 sheets of each color)
marker
12′ clothesline
60 clothespins

Steps:

1. Reproduce the clothes patterns on pages 46 and 47 and cut them out. Using six different colors of construction paper, stack 10 sheets of each color in six piles. Trace a different pattern on the top sheet of each pile and cut out 10 copies.

2. On each pattern of one color, write an article, a possessive pronoun, or a pronoun. Write the same word on both sides, but capitalize the first letter only on one side.

3. On a second color, write nouns. This time write one noun on the front and a different one on the back.

4. The third and fourth colors are for verbs. On each pattern, write one verb on the front and the same verb in a different tense on the back.

5. The fifth color is for adjectives, two to a pattern, one on front and a different one on back.

6. The last color is for closing punctuation. Draw a period or exclamation mark on each side of the pattern.

7. Hang a 12′ clothesline and pin all of the clothing pieces in random order onto it with clothespins.

8. Ask children to help you make sentences by rearranging the words pinned to the clothesline.

9. When all the pieces of clothing have been arranged into sentences, turn the pieces around (children may help you), reverse the line, or reposition the children and ask them to make new sentences, using the new words.

Variation:

In a corner of the room, hang the clothesline with the words pinned to it. Allow children to arrange the clothing pieces, independently, to form sentences.

Writing Skills
Making Sentences

SENTENCE CLOTHESLINE GAME
Patterns

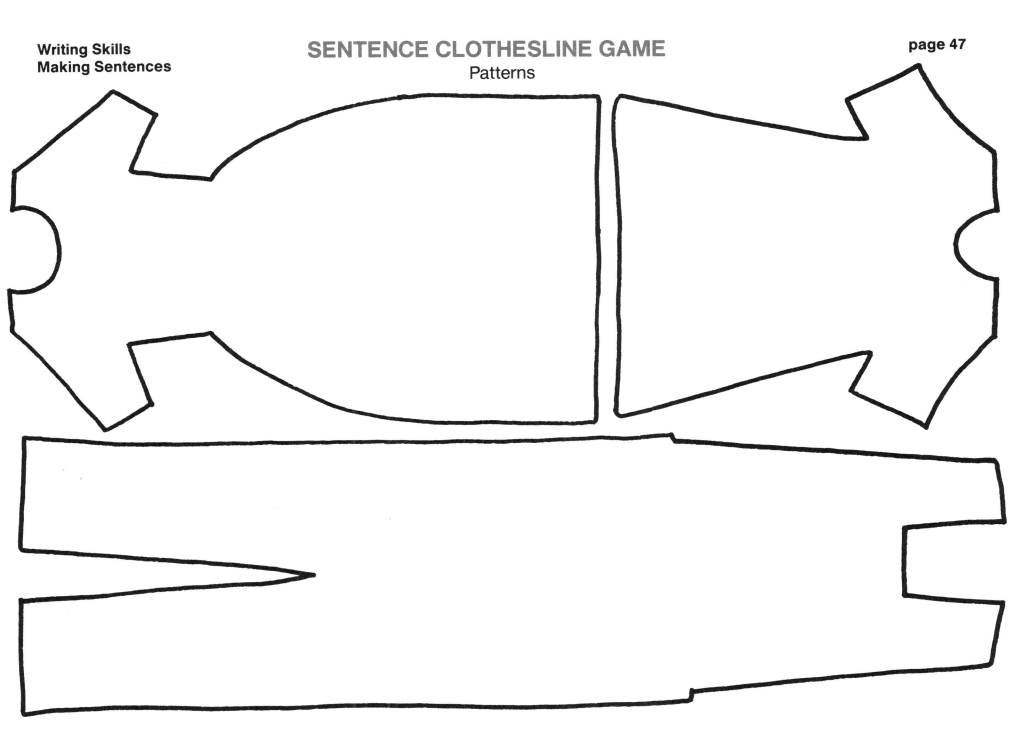

THE SILLY SENTENCES GAME
Classroom Game

Use the game described below to give your students practice in arranging articles, subjects, and verbs to make simple, silly sentences.

You need: sentence cards on pages 49, 50, and 51
glue
oaktag or lightweight cardboard
scissors

Steps:

1. Reproduce the 60 sentence cards on pages 49, 50, and 51. (Since this is a game for groups of six children, you may want to make several complete sets of cards.)

2. Mount each page of sentence cards on oaktag or lightweight cardboard, and cut them apart.

3. Divide your class into groups of six, and distribute a complete set of sentence cards to each group. (If your class does not divide evenly, each group may consist of five or seven children.)

4. Shuffle the 60 sentence cards, and give five cards to each child.

5. Place the remaining cards in the center of the play area so that children may draw from this pile.

6. Ask the children to look at the five cards they are holding. Each child who can form a sentence with three of the cards should set aside these three cards and draw three new ones from the pile. Each player may do this once before the game begins.

7. The youngest child in each group goes first. The first player takes a card from the draw pile in the center. If that player can form a sentence, he or she should read aloud the sentence, set aside the three cards, and draw three new ones. Only one sentence may be formed each turn. The player then discards one card, facedown, beside the draw pile.

8. Play continues clockwise until all of the cards in the draw pile have been used. The players then count up the number of sentences they have formed. The player who has made the greatest number of sentences wins. (In the case of a tie, shuffle the cards in the discard pile, form a new draw pile, and allow play to continue until all of the cards in the new draw pile have been used.)

Variation:

Create sentence cards on your own by writing articles, subjects, and verbs on individual index cards. For older children, add individual cards with prepositions, adjectives, conjunctions, and so on.

The	The	The	The	The
A	A	A	A	A
This	This	This	This	This
That	That	That	That	That

bear | dog | cat | mouse | lion

boy | girl | man | woman | bird

bug | frog | rabbit | monkey | clown

butterfly | worm | pig | monster | horse

runs.	hops.	cries.	laughs.	walks.
swims.	roars.	plays.	leaps.	jumps.
flies.	crawls.	eats.	talks.	hides.
sleeps.	sings.	smiles.	claps.	works.

CREATE A CLASS STORY
Storytelling / Art Project

After a field trip, class party, or other special class event, use these activities to help strengthen children's storytelling abilities.

You need: tape recorder
and blank tape
drawing paper
crayons

Optional: dark marker
chart paper
lined writing paper
pencils

Steps:

1. Following a field trip or special classroom activity, begin a discussion with children about their experience. Encourage children to use descriptive words and to indicate the sequence of events.

2. As the children tell about their experience, write their comments on the chalkboard.

3. When the children have completed the story to their satisfaction, copy the final version on chart paper. If desired, older children may copy the story onto lined writing paper.

4. Then have children repeat the story as you record it on a tape recorder. Let each child tell some part of the story.

5. Give each child a piece of drawing paper and some crayons. Ask each child to illustrate a part of the story, leaving a blank space at the bottom of the paper where a caption can be written.

6. When their drawings are finished, have each child write a sentence in the blank space. Younger children can dictate their sentences. Post the pictures on a bulletin board.

7. Then play the recorded story back for the children. If desired, children from another class may be invited to hear the story, or parents can listen to the tape when they visit the classroom.

You need: pictures on page 54
scissors
9″ × 12″ white construction paper
paste
pencils
pushpins or thumbtacks

Steps:

1. Make several copies of the pictures on page 54.

2. Cut the pictures into strips along the dotted lines.

3. Give each child a 9″ × 12″ piece of white construction paper. Show children how to fold their papers into six boxes. Papers should be positioned horizontally. (If desired, you may fold papers before handing them out to the children.)

4. Then give each child a strip of three pictures.

5. Ask children to cut their pictures apart and arrange them so that they tell a story. Have each child place the pictures on the paper, putting the picture that comes first in the story on the top left box of the paper, the second picture in the top middle box, and the last picture in the top right box. Quickly check each child's paper to see that the pictures are arranged properly. Children will then paste the pictures in place from left to right.

6. Each child will write a simple sentence in the box below each picture that tells what is happening. If children have questions as they work, have them raise their hands to signal you. (Younger children may dictate their sentences to you.)

7. When children have finished their sentences, let them color in the pictures. Then allow children to read their stories to the class. The pictures and stories can then be posted on a bulletin board.

The bird makes her nest.

The bird sits on the nest.

The bird feeds her baby.

Variation:

Cut out cartoons or comic strips from your local Sunday newspaper. Cut the comic strips apart, and ask children to paste the different frames in order onto a sheet of construction paper. Then have children write simple sentences beneath each frame to **make** their own dialogue for or descriptions of the comic-strip story. (Younger children may dictate the sentences to you.)

Reproduce and distribute the worksheet on the following page. Read aloud the story below to your class. Tell children to listen carefully to the story so that they can successfully travel through the maze to find the lost teddy bear.

SAMANTHA SNOOP was a private detective. She was very good at finding things that no one else could find. So when Bobby Jones could not find his teddy bear, he went right to Samantha Snoop for help.

"A lost teddy bear, hmmmmm. Well, the only thing to do is begin at the beginning. Let's see what clues we can find at your house, Bobby." So they hurried to Bobby Jones's front door, and, sure enough, Samantha spotted some very large paw prints. She and Bobby followed the paw prints until they ended, right at Bertie Bulldog's dog-house. As Samantha peered inside, out popped Bertie Bulldog. "What do you want?" he growled.

"We're looking for Bobby Jones's teddy bear, Bertie. Do you know where it might be or who might have taken it?"

"Of course not," barked Bertie. "The only thing I know is that a white, furry creature hopped by here not more than two hours ago. Why don't you chase the real culprits and leave a tired watchdog in peace!"

Samantha turned to Bobby and said, "On to the next clue, Bobby. We'll just have to follow the footprints from Bertie's house." So Samantha and Bobby carefully followed the tiny paw prints until they came to a rabbit's hole.

Samantha peeked into the dark entrance, and out popped a sleepy-looking rabbit.

"What do you want?" asked the rabbit, with a big yawn.

"We're looking for Bobby Jones's teddy bear. Do you know anything about this, Rabbit?"

"All I know is that someone with very tiny feet ran right by my hole not more than an hour ago, and splashed mud in my face! Whoever it was woke me up, too." And with that, the rabbit popped back into its hole.

"Well, Bobby, it looks like we're on the right track," said Samantha. "Let's follow these tiny footprints and see where they lead us." And they followed the tiny footprints, right to a rickety, rundown old house.

"Aha!" said Samantha. "I think we're on the right track."

Samantha knocked at the door, but no one answered. Then she noticed that there were tiny footprints leading away from the back of the house.

"Come on, Bobby," she cried. And they hurried along, following the tiny footprints, which led them to the back door of . . . Bobby Jones's house.

"Oh my," cried Bobby.

There, against the door, lay Bobby's teddy bear, with a note pinned to his little vest. And the note said, "I found this lonely teddy bear under a nearby tree. I hope this is where it belongs."

Bobby hugged his teddy bear to his chest, and turned to thank Samantha for all of her help. But Samantha was already on her way, for she had lots more mysteries to solve that day.

Listen to the story of Samantha Snoop.
Follow the footprints to find out where to find Bobby's lost teddy bear.

Name _____

WHAT'S THE STORY?
Art Project / Drawing Conclusions

The activity below can give children practice writing brief stories and drawing conclusions from story illustrations.

You need: worksheets on pages 58 and 59
pencils
crayons
scissors
12″ × 9″ construction paper
(one sheet per child)
glue

Steps:

1. Reproduce the worksheets on pages 58 and 59. Distribute the worksheets to the class.

2. Ask the children to look carefully at each story strip and figure out what is happening. Then have the children write a sentence describing what is happening in each frame.

3. Allow children to draw and color in the last frame of each strip with a picture that shows how the story ends. Have children write a brief sentence describing the ending they have chosen for the story.

4. Ask children to color in the whole story strip.

5. Once children have completed their story strips, have them cut apart the different strips.

6. To make a story-strip booklet, fold a 12″ × 9″ piece of construction paper in half, widthwise. Then fold it into thirds, lengthwise. Cut the paper in half, along the widthwise fold.

7. Have the children glue their three-frame story strips onto the folded sheets of construction paper.

8. Help them fold the strips, accordion style, leaving a blank panel at the front. Then tell the children to give their story strips a title and to write the title and/or draw a cover picture for the front of their story-strip booklets.

Follow-up Activity:

After they have completed their story strips, allow the children to share them with the class, comparing the similarities and differences of the descriptions and the endings they have chosen.

Look carefully at the pictures in the first row. On the lines beneath each one, write a sentence telling what is going on in that picture. In the last box, draw a picture that shows how the story ends, and write a sentence that tells about the ending. Do the same thing for the second row.

Name_____

_____

_____

_____

_____

WHAT'S THE STORY?
Worksheet

Look carefully at the pictures in the first row. On the lines beneath each one, write a sentence telling what is going on in that picture. In the last box, draw a picture that shows how the story ends, and write a sentence that tells about the ending. Do the same thing for the second row.

Name_____

_____
_____

_____
_____

_____
_____

_____
_____

_____
_____

_____
_____

THE FOX AND THE STORK
Aesop's Fable

Read the story below to your class. Then ask them the discussion questions about the story elements *Who*, *What*, *Where*, *When*, and *Why*. Reproduce the worksheet on the following page and distribute one to each child, to reinforce the elements and sequence of events in the story.

A LONG time ago, when the world was young, a wily fox invited a stork to have dinner with him. The stork accepted the fox's invitation and arrived at the fox's den just in time for dinner. The fox, who liked to play tricks on the other animals in the forest, had prepared only a very thin soup in a shallow dish. The fox was able to lap up the soup with great pleasure, but the stork was unable to eat a thing. She could only peck at the thin broth in the shallow dish with her long, thin beak, but she couldn't get a single drop in her mouth. At the end of the dinner, the stork was just as hungry as she had been when she began.

As the stork was getting ready to leave the fox's den, the fox expressed his great regret that his guest had eaten so little.

"I fear, dear stork, you do not like the way I season my food. I hope the soup was not distasteful to you," said the fox with a sly grin.

"Please do not apologize, friend fox. I have had a most interesting evening. Will you do me the honor to return the visit and dine with me one week from now?" replied the stork.

The fox agreed.

At the appointed time, the fox arrived at the stork's home. They sat down to eat, and the stork ordered the specially prepared broth to be brought to the table. To his surprise, the fox discovered that it was served in a long-necked jar with a narrow mouth. The stork eagerly thrust her long bill deep into the jar and enjoyed the delicious broth immensely. The fox had to content himself with licking the neck of the jar, for he could not fit his stubby snout inside to lap up the broth.

As the fox was making his goodbyes with as much good grace as he could muster, the stork said with a wry smile, "I do hope you do not expect me to apologize to you for the dinner *I* have served *you* tonight."

And the fox slunk away into the forest, with the sound of the stork's laughter echoing in his ears.

Discussion Questions:

1. Who was this story about?

2. When did this story take place?

3. Where does this story take place?

4. What happens in this story?

5. Why does the fox invite the stork to dinner? Why does the stork return the invitation?

THE FOX AND THE STORK
Worksheet

Cut apart the pictures along the dotted lines. On a blank piece of paper,
put the pictures in order and glue them in place. Color the pictures.
Then write a short sentence that tells what is going on in each one.

Name_____

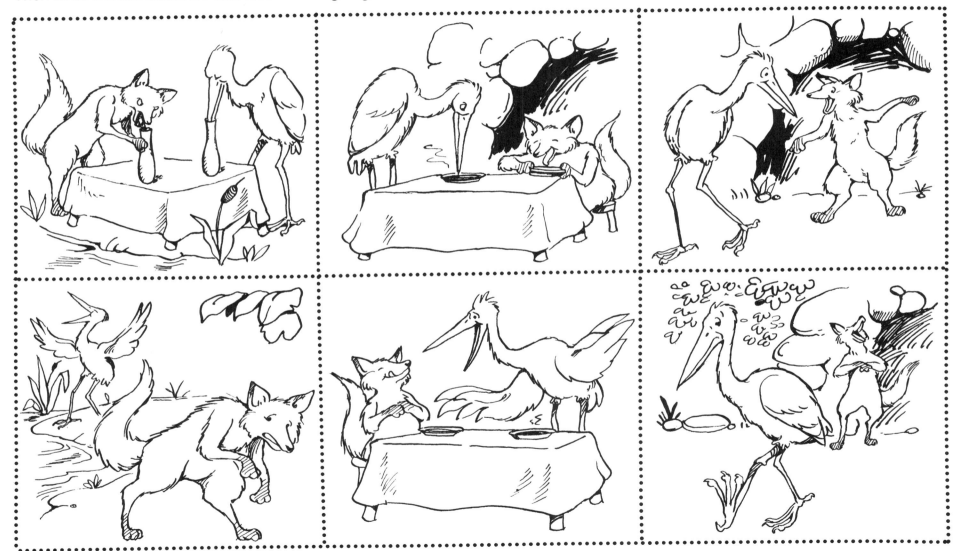

MAKE A MOVIE MACHINE
Art Project

Use the movie machine described below in conjunction with the classroom movie strip
suggested on page 63.

You need: sturdy cardboard box (approximately
14½" wide × 12¾" long × 9½" deep)
pencil
ruler
sharp knife, scissors, or razor blade
2 wooden dowel sticks (¾" diameter and
18" long)
movie strip on shelf paper (see page 63)
clear tape

Steps:

1. In the center of the wider side of a sturdy cardboard box, mark off an 11" × 9" rectangle. Leave a 1½" to 1¾" border from the rim of the box on all sides. (Make sure the flaps of the box open at the top.)

2. Using a sharp knife, scissors, or razor blade, cut out the 11" × 9" rectangle to make the opening for the movie screen.

3. On each of the narrower sides of the box, mark off a ¾" square, 2" in from the side on which you have cut out the screen and 2" down from the top of the box. Then mark off another ¾" square below it, 2" in from the screen side of the box and 2" up from the bottom of the box. Cut out all four squares. (These are the openings through which the dowel sticks will be inserted.)

4. Insert one dowel through the two top squares and the other dowel through the bottom two squares. Center the dowel sticks so that approximately 2" of each side extend through the openings, so that the movie strip can be unrolled easily.

5. With a pencil, mark the midpoint of each dowel. At the top edge of the roll of shelf paper, mark the center of the paper.

6. When the story illustrations have been taped, in sequence, on the roll of shelf paper, match the center of the shelf paper to the center of the top dowel stick, and tape the edge of the shelf paper to the top dowel stick.

7. Carefully roll the shelf paper onto the top dowel stick by turning the stick slowly and evenly.

8. When you reach the end of the shelf paper, center it according to the midpoint marked on the bottom dowel stick, and tape the shelf paper to it.

9. Carefully roll the shelf paper in reverse onto the bottom dowel stick until you get to the beginning of the film strip.

CLASSROOM MOVIE STRIP
Art Project / Storytelling

Use the activity suggested below to teach children the elements of a story
and how to organize the story elements into a logical sequence.

You need: sheets of white paper (8½″ × 11″),
one for each child
crayons or colored markers
clear tape
roll of shelf paper (13″ × 16⅔ yds.)
movie machine on page 62

Steps:

1. Explain to the class that together they are going to create a story.

2. On the chalkboard, list the following questions: Who? When? Where? What? Why? As the children determine the story elements, write their answers beneath each question.

3. Ask the children *who* their story will include: a princess? a prince? a dragon? a monster? a creature from outer space? a wizard? a witch?

4. Once the children have chosen the characters, have them determine *when* the story takes place: past? present? future? Then ask children *where* the story takes place: an imaginary kingdom? an unknown planet? another part of the real world?

5. After these elements have been determined, begin the story for the class by using the answers to Who? When? and Where? Then have each child contribute a sentence that adds to the story. Each time a new aspect or detail is added, write it down beneath the What? Why? or other appropriate question words. Point out to the children the category in which their sentence belongs, and that each sentence should build on the one that precedes it. Number the sentences to help the children sequence the illustrations.

6. After children have completed the story, distribute sheets of 8½″ × 11″ white paper.

7. Each child can illustrate details of the story. For example, one child can draw a picture of the main character, another can illustrate the place, others can illustrate the additional characters and the events that occur.

8. The notes you have written on the chalkboard can help children to sequence the illustrations. Once the class has decided on the sequence, tape the illustrations, in order, to a roll of shelf paper. (You may want to tape a title page or sheet of paper entitled "Beginning" to the first frame.)

9. Then follow the instructions on page 62 to construct a movie machine. Once it has been set up, retell the class story as you unroll the illustrations on the movie machine.

Variation:

1. You may want to record the class story and play the tape recording while the illustrations are unrolled on the movie screen.

2. For older children, have each one make up his or her own story, and display individual stories on the screen.

You need: glue
story starter cards (see below)
scissors
manila envelope

Optional: clear plastic adhesive tape

To Prepare the Story Starter Cards:

1. On a 3" x 5" index card, write a couple of sentences that could be the start of a story. For example: "When our class went to the zoo, the animals began to talk. I was surprised when..."; "When I was cleaning the basement, I found a secret tunnel. I stepped inside and..."; "One day on the playground, I swung so high that the swing didn't come back down. Instead..." You might draw a picture on each card as well. Create about 24 different story starter cards.

2. Laminate the cards or cover them with clear plastic adhesive.

3. Place the story starter cards in a manila envelope.

To Use the Story Starter Cards:

For younger children:

1. Divide the class into groups of four or five children each.

2. Let one child from each group draw a story starter card from the envelope.

3. Read each group's card to the children in that group. Give the groups about five minutes to create brief stories based on their story starter cards.

4. Have each group, in turn, go to the front of the class and tell their stories aloud to their classmates, with each group member narrating a part of the story.

For older children:

1. Give each child a pencil and a piece of writing paper.

2. Ask each child to select a story starter card from the envelope.

3. Each child will write an original story based on the selected card. The children's stories should contain at least five sentences each.

4. When children have finished writing their stories, they may read them aloud to the class.

Variations:

1. For younger classes, give each child a story starter card. Ask each child to invent a story based on the card and, on a blank piece of paper, to draw a picture of how the story ends. Let the child dictate the story's ending to you. Then post the story starter cards and the children's illustrated story endings on a bulletin board.

2. With older classes, select one story starter card and read it to the children. Have each child write a brief story (five or six sentences long) based on the card. Then ask each child to read his or her story to the class to see how many different tales can be created from one idea.

3. Children may use the story starter cards to motivate them when they make class movie strips in the "Classroom Movie Strip" activity described on page 63.